TALES
of .
TRILUSSA

Translated from the Romanesco
by John DuVal

TALES
of
TRILUSSA

Carlo
Alberto
Salustri

The University of Arkansas Press
Fayetteville   London
1990

Manufactured in the United States of America
94 93 92 91 90   5 4 3 2 1

Designer *Ch H Russell*
Typeface *Linotron 202 Weiss*

The paper used in this publication meets the minimum re-
quirements of the American National Standard for Perma-
nence of Paper for Printed Library Materials Z39 48-1984
⊚

Library of Congress Cataloging-in-Publication Data

Trilussa, 1871–1950
    Tales of Trilussa / Carlo Alberto Salustri   translated from
the Romanesco by John DuVal
        p   cm
    English and Italian
    Includes bibliographical references (p   )
    ISBN 1-55728-150-5 (alk paper)
    ISBN 1-55728-151-3 (pbk alk paper)
    1 Trilussa, 1871–1950—Translations, English
I DuVal, John, 1940–   II Title
PQ4841 A46T35   1990
851' 8—dc20   89-20696
                                                        CIP

For Kay, Kathleen, Niell, and Hélène, with love.

Acknowledgments

Grateful acknowledgment is made to Arnoldo Mondadori Editori for permission to publish the originals and translations of Trilussa's poems.

Grateful acknowledgment is also made to *Mundus Artium* for permission to publish "Force of Habit" and "Happiness," and to *Poetry World* for permission to publish "Happiness."

I would like to thank Fulbright College of the University of Arkansas for a Research Incentive Grant to go to Rome in the summer of 1984 to do a preliminary study of Trilussa's poetry, and for a further Research Incentive Grant in the fall of 1987 to work on this and other projects.

I would like to thank Giorgio Roberti, director of the Centro Romanesco Trilussa, for his long talks with me in Rome on Romanesco, Trilussa's life, and Trilussa's poetry. I would like to thank Fortunato Pasqualino for his kindness to me in Rome and for our conversations about Trilussa and about Italian, Romanesco, and American literature. I also would like to thank Meo Carbone and Gina Agostinelli for their warm hospitality in Rome, for arranging for me to meet Giorgio Roberti, and for their good work in helping to get the translation rights for Trilussa's poetry.

I would like to thank Miller Williams for introducing me to the above-mentioned friends. I would also like to thank him for introducing me to Trilussa and his poetry, for advising, encouraging, and urging me to do better. I would also like to thank Johnny Danti, Rina Ferrarelli, Louise Rosier, and Olivia

Sordo for their patience and good work in making the Romanesco clearer to me and for the respect they showed to both Trilussa and me in demanding better translations I would like to thank all the people whom I met in Italy for their high regard for Trilussa and for their encouragement

Contents

Introduction

In the summer of 1887, fifteen-year-old Carlo Alberto Salustri, "dressed in his Sunday best, nervous but resolute,"[1] walked into the editorial office of the Romanesco newspaper *Il Rugantino* and offered the editor one hand-written sonnet. It was accepted and published under the single name, Trilussa, an anagram of his last name that the young author had chosen for a pseudonym. Thus began a career that would last sixty-seven years. This sonnet and others in *Il Rugantino* soon established Trilussa as the foremost Romanesco poet of his time.

The geographical center of Romanesco is Trastevere, Rome beyond the Tiber, to which the Romans had retreated after the barbarian invasions. Unlike modern Italian, which descends from the Florentine of Petrarch and Dante, the Romanesco language claims direct descent from the Latin of the Romans. Before Trilussa, Romanesco's claim to literary glory rested mainly upon the achievement of the Romanesco sonneteer, G. G. Belli.

Nothing could be less Petrarchan than Belli's sonnets. Cramming story after story into the short, traditionally unnarrative sonnet, Belli had subjected life on the Roman streets, Papal grandeur and corruption, and God Himself to the harsh scrutiny of a language that had little patience with metaphysical musing. The Romanesco literary tradition, continued in many Trastevere journals, was largely a continuation of Belli's transformation of the sonnet, with its often

1. Gennaro Vaccaro, *Vocabolario romanesco trilussiano* (Rome: Romana Libri Alfabeto, 1971), 15.

sarcastic, often wryly comic voice, fierce honesty, and natu-
ralistic detail To these characteristics Trilussa added a differ-
ent kind of comic-lyric sensibility, influenced by the late
nineteenth-century Italian Crepuscolari poets and the popu-
lar canzonette sung in the Roman streets and dance halls

Trilussa's first volume of poems, *Stelle de Roma* (*Stars of
Rome*), descriptions of the beautiful women of Rome, came
out in 1889 This volume he never allowed to be reprinted,
but the many volumes of sonnets, fables, satires, and lyrics
that followed were reprinted again and again His satire ex-
posed the pomposity and double-talk of everyone from street
thugs to cabinet ministers The fascists, when they took
power in 1922, were no exception, except that there was a
new element to satirize in the new regime terror Such
poems as "In the Shade" and "The Last of the Bogeyman" be-
come increasingly complex when we realize that they them-
selves make their author more vulnerable to the terror they
mock During the hearings after the war, when he was intro-
duced as "the anti-fascist" poet, Trilussa corrected "Not ex-
actly; I was simply not a fascist"[2] This was true His direct
criticism of the fascists had been no more frequent than his
criticism of other political parties before the takeover, but it
had been dangerous

By this time, despite the fact that he was a "dialect" poet,
Trilussa was a poet of national and international standing
From 1922 on, the Milan-based Mondadori Press was pub-
lishing and distributing his works all over Italy He was one
of those extremely rare poets who have made their living en-
tirely from their own work, which, in his case, was sold to
magazines, published in books, and recited on his many
speaking engagements By the time of his death in 1950,
many of his poems had been translated into English, Spanish,
Portuguese, French, Romanian, Italian, and two Italian
dialects

2 Trilussa, *Tutte le poesie,* ed Pietro Gibellini (Milan Mondadori,
1969), 22

2

Just three weeks before his death in December 1950, the Italian Parliament named Trilussa, by acclamation, Senator for Life. Trilussa is said to have appreciated the irony. Nevertheless, his was a rare honor, reserved for "those who through their eminent services or merits have brought honor to the Fatherland." Only Alessandro Manzoni (1860) and Giovanni Verga (1920) had received it solely on the basis of literary merit. Senator Vittorio Emanuele Orlanda, in an address to the Senate a few days after Trilussa's death, perhaps best sums up the feelings that led to Trilussa's nomination:

> He was very precious to me, not only for his great worth as an artist, but also because of the tenderness and strength with which he upheld my faith during times when, if I looked around me, I could feel myself wavering. We who remained here [rather than going into exile] formed a small Freemasonry. . . . Well, Trilussa not only was one of us, but he gave us courage and cured us of our scepticism· he remained on his feet, to the honor of Italian intellectual life, so that it could not be said that it completely failed [3]

Trilussa's collected poetry, *Tutte le poesie*, published in 1951, sold out within a few days. Three editions sold out within a year. It has now been through twenty-eight printings, and his selected poems, *Poesie Scelte*, published in two volumes in 1969, is now in its seventeenth printing. Traveling in Italy, I have met people on the train and in guesthouses, not only from Rome, but from Genoa, Florence, and Sicily, who were fondly familiar with his work. Some even honored me with recitations of poems. So he remains a very popular poet in Italy, although he is little known in English.

Poems in this volume are in the same order as they appear in *Tutte le poesie*. All originals are from *Tutte le poesie* except for "Epigramma," which is from Luigi Barzini's *The Italians*.

3 Maria Teresa Russo, from "Atti Parlamentari" (Discuss Senato, dicembre 1950) in "Trilussa senatore," *Studi trilussiani* (Rome: Instituto di Studi Romani, 1977)

3

ER VENTRILOCO

Se credi a questo, sei 'no scemo, scusa
pô sta' che un omo parli co' la gente
come se ne la panza internamente
ciavesse quarche machina arinchiusa?

Nun credo che in un'epoca che s'usa
d'aprì la bocca senza di' mai gnente
esista 'sto fenomeno vivente
che dice tante cose a bocca chiusa!

Parla cór ventre! Oh questa sì ch'è bella!
Sortanto er poveraccio che nun magna
se sente fa' glu-glu ne le budella
Io stesso, speciarmente a fin de mese,
me sento che lo stomaco se lagna
Ma sai ched'è? La voce der Paese!

1919

$\mathcal{V}$ENTRILOQUIST

Ventriloquist means *stomach speaker*. It's Latin.
If you believe in him, by God, you're gullible—
as if the stomach were a place to chat in
or speech could come from swallowing a syllable.

I can't believe that in an age like ours
when everybody's mouth is open, but—but—
when nothing is said, anyone's got the power
of saying anything with his mouth shut.

His stomach talk? What is he trying to tell me?
Only a poor beggar who hasn't once
eaten today hears "glub glub" in his belly.
Matter of fact, especially when the month's
almost out, my guts grumble and grate.
Know whose voice it is? The voice of the State!

1919

ƐR TEPPISTA A LA DIMOSTRAZZIONE

Li sassi che volaveno per aria
cascaveno de peso tra le file
de li sordati, verdi pe' la bile
de conservà la carma necessaria

Come vôi che sparassero? Er fucile
che mira su la crasse proletaria
è un'infamia, un sopruso, una barbaria
che fa vergogna a un popolo civile!

E pe' questo tiravo! A un polizzotto
je detti un sércio in testa e je strillai
«Impunito! Bojaccia! Galeotto!»
Era precisamente er brigadiere
che m'arestò quer giorno sur tranvai
perché fregai l'orloggio a un forastiere

THE HOODLUM AT THE DEMONSTRATION

Rocks and cobblestones and bricks rained
and thundered down and fell around the file
of guardsmen, green from choking down the bile,
straining to keep a stoical restraint.

You think they'll shoot? No. Any gun
pointed at the proletariat
means outrage, police brutality, the rights
of the people crushed, and freedom trampled on.

That's why I was down there making a racket
and throwing stones at policemen. I took aim
and beaned one. "Spy!" I yelled. "Pig! Stoogie! Bully!
Tool of the bourgeoisie!" (This was the same
cop that had nabbed me when I was on the trolley
lifting a wallet from a tourist's pocket.)

LA RISATA DE LA DUCHESSA

Lei ce pretenne pe' li denti bianchi
apposta quanno parla co' quarcuno
sbotta certe risate, sarvognuno,
da méttese le mano su li fianchi¹

Ride   ma badi a lei che nu' la sbianchi
perché finora nu' lo sa nessuno
che l'ha pagati trenta lire l'uno,
che la dentiera costa mille franchi¹

Ma l'ho scoperta io, che se la sciacqua
prima de pijà sonno¹ io l'ho scoperta
quanno la mette drento ar bicchier d'acqua¹
E a me me fa 'st'effetto certe sere
lei dorme, e la dentiera a bocca aperta
seguita a ride sola ner bicchiere

THE DUCHESS'S LAUGHTER

The lady that I work for sure takes pride
in her straight teeth. She's got a way of conversing
that shows the pearly whites to any person
she talks to. Then she laughs and holds her sides.

She laughs a lot—but wouldn't she be cursing
if she thought anybody knew the truth—
truth is, she bought them, thirty lire a tooth,
a thousand francs for the entire insertion.

And I'm the one who knows the truth about her,
because I've watched her in the night and caught her
rinsing her teeth out in a glass she keeps
beside her bed. Later, while she sleeps,
sometimes I look in and I get the creeps—
her dentures keep on laughing in the water.

ER PORCO E ER SOMARO

Una matina un povero Somaro,
ner vede un Porco amico annà ar macello,
sbottò in un pianto e disse —Addio, fratello
nun se vedremo più, nun c'è riparo!

—Bisogna esse filosofo, bisogna
—je disse er Porco—via, nun fa' lo scemo,
ché forse un giorno se ritroveremo
in quarche mortadella de Bologna!

THE PIG AND THE DONKEY

A poor, lean donkey stood and watched his friend,
the pig, hauled to the slaughterhouse. "Dear brother!"
the donkey brayed, "farewell, farewell. It's over.
We'll never meet again. This is the end!"

The pig replied, "Now, don't act like an ass.
Be philosophical: life is a passage.
For all we know it may yet come to pass
we'll meet again in some bologna sausage."

L'OMO E ER SERPENTE

Un Omo che dormiva in mezzo a un prato
s'insognò che una donna tanto bella
l'aveva abbraccicato
Naturarmente, l'Omo, ner vedella,
fece un gran sarto e se svejò ma, invece
de trovà a quella, vidde ch'un Serpente
je s'era intorcinato intorno ar collo
a rischio de strozzallo come un pollo
—Ah, sei tu? Meno male!
Me credevo de peggio!—disse l'Omo
mentre se storcinava l'animale
Ma ciarimase tanto impressionato
che da quer giorno cominciò a confonne
li serpenti e le donne Tant'è vero
che un'antra notte, mentre s'insognava
d'avé ar collo 'na vipera davero,
trovò la moje che l'abbraccicava

THE MAN AND THE SNAKE

A man, sleeping in a field one night,
dreamed a lovely woman came and kissed
and held him tight
As soon as he realized that she was pressed
close against his skin, he jumped and woke.
But she was gone. Instead, he found a snake
wrapped around his neck, ready to choke
him like a chicken.
"Oh, you? You I can take!
It could have been worse. Lordy, Lordy!"
And he unwrapped the snake from around his body.
But he was so affected by that experience
that he could never again keep his serpents
and his women straight. So when another night
he had a dream in which a snake found him
in his own bed, he woke up to find
his wife awake, putting her arms around him.

L'ORTOLANO E ER DIAVOLO

C'era 'na vorta un povero Ortolano
che, se j'annava un pelo a l'incontrario,
dava de piccio a tutto er calennario,
metteva in ballo er paradiso sano,
Dio guardi! cominciava a biastimà
—Corpo de   ! sangue de   ! managgia la   !

Un giorno, mentre stava a tajà un cavolo
e che pe' sbajo tajò invecce un broccolo,
come faceva sempre attaccò un moccolo
però, 'sta vorta, scappò fòra er Diavolo
che l'agguantò da dove l'impiegati
cianno li pantoloni più lograti

Ner sentisse per aria, straportato,
l'Ortolano diceva l'orazzione,
pregava le medesime persone
che poco prima aveva biastimato
—Dio! Cristo santo! Vergine Maria!
M'ariccommanno a voi! Madonna mia!—

Er Diavolo, a sti' nomi, è naturale
che aprì la mano e lo lassò de botto
l'Ortolano cascò, come un fagotto,

14

THE GARDENER AND THE DEVIL

There was a gardener who was so bad tempered,
at the slightest screw up his complaints
punctured the vault of heaven and dismembered
God and a whole calendar of saints.
Damn! You should have heard his blaspheming fit:
"Body of—! Blood of—! Bones of—! Holy shit!"

One morning, when he pulled up cauliflower
by accident, thinking it was cabbage,
and he, as always, started to devour
the body of religion like a savage,
out popped the Devil from some cabbage plants
and seized him by the worn place on his pants.

When he found himself above the steeples
and moving fast, the gardener got busy redeeming
his life by calling out to the very people
that minutes earlier he had been blaspheming:
"Madonna Mary! Dear Lord Jesus! God!" he
beseeched, "into your hands I commend my body."

Sure enough those sweet names scared the hell
out of the Devil. He lost his grip, and down
plummeted the gardener. He fell

sopra un pajone senza fasse male
—L'ho avuta bona!—disse ner cascà—
Corpo de   ᛁ sangue de   ᛁ mannaggia la   ᛁ

into a rick of hay with no harm done.
"Wow, close," he said, "but I got out of it!
Body of—! Blood of—! Bones of—! Holy shit!"

ER MAESTRO DE MUSICA
E LA MOSCA

Un celebre Maestro
era rimasto nun se sa si quanti
giorni dell'anno co' la penna in mano
e la carta de musica davanti
per aspettà che je venisse l'estro
ma, spreme spreme, nun j'usciva gnente
Ècchete che un ber giorno
una Mosca zozzona e impertinente
agnede franca franca
sopra la carta bianca,
e je ce fece tanti punti neri
come quelli che spesso avrete visto
ne le vetrine de li pasticceri
—Chi sà—disse er Maestro—che 'sta Mosca,
che m'ha messo 'sti segni, nun conosca
le note de la musica? Chissà
che lei, senza volello, m'abbia fatto
er pezzo der prim'atto?
Questo è un *do*, questo è un *re, si, si, la, fa*   —
E du' o tre vorte lo provò ar pianforte
Er motivo era bello, e da quer giorno,
quanno la Mosca je volava intorno,
nu' je faceva sciò, nu' la cacciava
anzi, er più de le vorte, se ciaveva

THE MUSIC MAESTRO
AND THE FLY

A maestro of great reputation,
cloistered in his room for days and days
year after year, holding his pen in hand,
nervously poised above the page,
waited for inspiration.
He squeezed and squeezed, but still he brought forth
    nothing,
till one fine day
an impudent housefly came buzzing,
boldly put its feet
on the white sheet,
and deposited little dots
like the ones flies do in pastry shops.
"It's possible," the maestro said, "the fly
that marked this sheet knows more than meets the eye
of musical notation. Could it be
without intending it, this fly composed
a good motif? Who knows?
This is a do, a re, sol, sol, and la fa mi. . . ."
He tried it once on the piano. Nice—
The melody was good. That's how it was:
from that day on, when the fly would buzz
around the room, he wouldn't shoo it out.
If he had anything sweet,

er zucchero o er candito, je lo dava
pe' fasse fa' più punti che poteva
Ma una matina, invece
de falli su la carta, je li fece
sopra a certe camice innammidate
portate allora da la stiratrice
Che vôi sentì er Maestro! Era un ossesso!
—Brutta porca che sei! Brutta vassalla!
Chi t'ha imparato a fa' 'ste zozzerie
su le camice mie?—
E je coreva appresso p'acchiappalla
La Mosca allora j'arispose male,
dice —Vojantri séte tutti eguale
ammazza ammazza, tutti d'una razza
Nun fate caso a certe puzzonate
finché ve fanno commodo, ma quanno
capite che ve possino fa' danno,
diventate puliti, diventate!
Io, invece de chiamalla pulizzia,
la chiamerebbe con un antro nome   —
Però la Mosca nu' je disse come
fece quattro puntini e scappò via

20

he'd smear enough about
to make the fly leave more specks on the sheet.
But one morning when the fly flitted
into the room, it missed the page and did it
on the Maestro's freshly laundered shirts.
You should have heard the Maestro yell and curse:
"Despicable insect! Filthy vermin! Drat!
How dare you come here scattering your crap
on my clean shirts!"
And then he charged the fly and *swat* and *swat*!
The fly was also quick. It answered back:
"You guys are all alike, your whole damn pack.
Kill, kill! that's all you're good for, kill, kill.
You don't notice scum
until it somehow turns to your advantage.
But when you realize it can do you damage,
look how hygenic you become—
except that I think *hygiene* is not
quite the word that such as you deserve."
He didn't say which word could better serve,
but he marked the shirt with another little dot.

ER GATTO E ER CANE

Un Gatto soriano
diceva a un Barbone.
—Nun porto rispetto
nemmanco ar padrone,
perché a l'occasione
je sgraffio la mano,
ma tu che lo lecchi
te becchi le bòtte
te mena, te sfotte,
te mette in catena
cór muso rinchiuso
e un cerchio cór bollo
sull'osso der collo
Seconno la moda
te taja li ricci,
te spunta la coda
Che belli capricci!
Io, guarda so' un Gatto,
so' un ladro, lo dico
ma a me nun s'azzarda
de famme 'ste cose   —
Er Cane rispose
—Ma io   je so' amico!

THE CAT AND THE DOG

The cat said to the dog,
"Look at it this way:
you'll never see me pay
any respect to the man.
In fact, if I'm in the mood,
I scratch him on the hand.
But you, you fetch his slippers,
lick his boots and slobber.
What does it get you? A kick!
He chains you to a stick
and chokes you with a collar,
or keeps you in a kennel,
then crimps your ears and tags you,
bobs your tail and clips you,
because it's the latest fad,
and, brother, you've been had!
Look at me: I'm a cat!
I've stolen again and again,
but the man's never tried
to keep me muzzled or penned."
The dog replied,
"But I'm his friend."

CORE DE TIGRE

'Na Tigre der serajo de Nummava,
come vidde tra er pubbrico 'na donna
che la guardava tanto, la guardava,
disse ar Leone —S'io incontrassi quella
in mezzo d'un deserto, e avessi fame,
mica la magnerebbe è troppo bella!
Io, invece, bona bona,
j'annerebbe vicino
come fa er cagnolino
quanno va a spasseggià co' la padrona —
La bella donna, intanto,
pensanno che cór manto
ce sarebbe venuto un ber tappeto,
disse ar marito che ciaveva accanto
—Io me la magno a furia de guardalla
che pelo! che colori! com'è bella!
Quanto me piacerebbe a scorticalla

TIGER'S HEART

A tiger in the Nouma-Hawa Zoo
looked at the crowd of people by his cage
and saw a lady looking him through and through.
He told the lion, "If I'd gone hungry for days
and found her in the desert, I'd take pity
and wouldn't eat her. She's too pretty.
I'd be good and I'd trot
beside her like Fido or Spot
walking with his owner in the city."
The beautiful lady, meanwhile, taking note
of how the tiger's coat
would make her a fine rug,
said to her husband (he was there with her),
"What colors! What stripes! What fur!
It seems a waste to have a tiger in it.
What a pleasure it would be to skin it."

ER COCCODRILLO

Ner mejo che un signore e 'na signora,
marito e moje, staveno sdrajati
su la riva der mare, scappò fòra
un Coccodrillo co' la boca aperta
e l'occhi spaventati
La moje, ch'era sverta,
s'aggiustò li riccetti e scappò via
mentre ch'er Coccodrillo, inviperito,
se masticava er povero marito
come magnasse un pollo a l'osteria
Siccome er Coccodrillo, per natura,
magna l'omo eppoi piagne, puro quello
se mésse a piagne come 'na cratura
Ogni cinque minuti
ciaripensava come li cornuti
e risbottava un antro piantarello
Tanto ch'er giorno appresso, a l'istess'ora,
ner rivedé la povera signora
riprincipiò le lagrime e li lagni,
sperava forse che s'intenerisse
ma invece, sì! La vedova je disse
—Dio mio, quanto sei scemo! Ancora piagni?

THE CROCODILE

A man and his wife lay down a little while
beside the sea, talking, laughing, lounging,
when, all of a sudden, a crocodile
rushed from the waters, jaws all agape
and eyes a-bulging.
The wife was in good shape.
She rearranged her dress and off she ran.
Meanwhile, the crocodile in a frenzy ate
every morsel of her unlucky mate
like a chicken dinner in a restaurant.
A crocodile by nature eats a man,
then bursts out crying, so that's what this one did
bawling and braying like a little kid,
fretting like a cuckold. On the quarter hour,
came another shower.
Next day and the same location,
seeing the lady near where he was lying,
the crocodile broke out in a lamentation
worse than before, weeping, wailing, eyeing
the widow to see if she'd join in. Instead,
she looked him in the eye. "Listen," she said,
"I can't believe this! Are you still crying?"

LA GUERRA

Ner mejo che un Sordato annava in guerra
er Cavallo je disse chiaramente
—Io nun ce vengo!—e lo buttò per terra
        precipitosamente

—No, nun ce vengo,—disse—e me ribbello
all'omo che t'ha messo l'odio in core
e te commanna de scannà un fratello
        in nome der Signore!

Io—dice—so' 'na bestia troppo nobbile
p'associamme a l'infamie che fai tu
se vôi la guerra vacce in automobbile,
        n'ammazzerai de più!

WAR

Riding off to war, a soldier heard
his horse speak clearly: "Hey, to hell with you!"
And then the horse suddenly reared and threw
                    the soldier in the dirt.

"I won't go," said the horse. "And I revolt
against the men who turned your heart to hate
and sent you off to cut your brother's throat
                    for Jesus Christ's sake.

I am too noble a beast. I've had my fill
of your atrocities. If you want war,
go in a car; that way you can kill
                    even more."

LA LIBBERTA DE PENSIERO

Un Gatto bianco, ch'era presidente
der circolo der Libbero Pensiero,
sentì che un Gatto nero,
libbero pensatore come lui,
je faceva la critica
riguardo a la politica
ch'era contraria a li principî sui
—Giacché nun badi a li fattacci tui,
—je disse er Gatto bianco inviperito—
rassegnerai le propie dimissione
e uscirai da le file der partito
ché qui la pôi pensà libberamente
come te pare a te, ma a condizzione
che t'associ a l'idee der presidente
e a le proposte de la commissione¹
—È vero, ho torto, ho aggito malamente   —
rispose er Gatto nero
E pe' restà ner Libbero Pensiero
da quela vorta nun pensò più gnente

FREEDOM OF THOUGHT

It was brought to the attention
of the white cat who was President
of the Free Thinkers' Convention
that another Free Thought tomcat, who was black,
had politicked
and preached ideas that happened to conflict
with certain principles the white cat backed.
"Your actions show you don't know how to act,"
the white cat snarled, "so listen here: I strip
your office from you; also your commission.
You're out of the party! Turn in your membership!
You're free to think—that's what we've always meant:
think anything you want, on the condition
your principles and thoughts are in accord
with statements and directives of the Board
and with the President."
"You're right. I was wrong. I meant no offense.
I take it back," said the black cat.
To stay a free thinker,
he didn't do any thinking after that.

L'AUTOMOBBILE E ER SOMARO

—Rottadecollo!—disse un Somarello
ner vede un Automobbile a benzina—
Indove passi tu nasce un macello!
Hai sbudellato un cane, una gallina,
un porco, un'oca, un pollo
Povere bestie! Che carneficina!
Che sfraggello che fai! Rottadecollo!
—Nun fiottà tanto, faccia d'impunito!
—rispose inviperito l'Automobbile—
Se vede che la porvere e lo sbuffo
de lo stantuffo t'hanno intontonito!
Nun sai che quann'io corro ciò la forza
de cento e più cavalli? E che te credi
che chi vô fa' cariera se fa scupolo
de quelli che se trova fra li piedi?
Io corro e me n'infischio, e nun permetto
che 'na bestiaccia ignobbile
s'azzardi de mancamme de rispetto!—
E ner di' 'ste parole l'Automobbile
ce mésso drento tanto mai calore
che er motore, infocato, je scoppiò
Allora cambiò tono Dice —E mó?
Chi me rimorchierà fino ar deposito?

THE CAR AND THE DONKEY

"Road Hog!" the donkey shouted at the big
automobile with the diesel-powered motor.
"Everywhere you go, it's a damn slaughter.
Already you've run over a pig,
a duck, a goose, two roosters, and a dog.
Poor creatures! You're nothing but a road hog!"
"All right, you silly squealer, what's the big deal?"
snorted the automobile.
"Apparently that long bonehead of yours
is rattled by dust, exhaust, and shifting gears.
Don't you realize I can cut loose with the force
of more than a hundred horses while you stay put?
What makes you think go-getters with careers
give a damn who's falling underfoot?
I run, and to hell with you. Know what you are?
You're a dumb ass! So don't you be
impudent when you're addressing me!"
All this while, the car
was getting worked up. It almost choked with rage.
It overheated, blew off steam, and stalled.
Now it changed its tune. "Hey there," it called,
"who wants to tow me to the next garage?

Amico mio, tu capiti a proposito,
tu solo pôi sarvà la situazzione
—Vengo,—je disse er Ciuccio—e me consolo
che cento e più cavalli a l'occasione
hanno bisogno d'un Somaro solo!

It's up to you, friend, to save the situation!"
"Well, okay," said the donkey, "it's some consolation
that more than a hundred horses, filled with gas,
sometimes need an ass."

LA MASCHERA

Vent'anni fa m'ammascherai pur'io!
E ancora tengo er grugno de cartone
che servì p'annisconne quello mio
Sta da vent'anni sopra un credenzone
quela Maschera buffa, che'è restata
sempre co' la medesima espressione,
sempre co' la medesima risata
Una vorta je chiesi —E come fai
a conservà lo stesso bon umore
puro ne li momenti der dolore,
puro quanno me trovo fra li guai?
Felice te, che nun te cambi mai!
Felice te, che vivi senza core!—
La Maschera rispose —E tu che piagni
che ce guadagni? Gnente! Ce guadagni
che la gente dirà Povero diavolo,
te compatisco   me dispiace assai
Ma, in fonno, credi, nun j'importa un cavolo!
Fa' invece come me, ch'ho sempre riso
e se te pija la malinconia
coprete er viso co' la faccia mia
così la gente nun se scoccerà   —
D'allora in poi nascónno li dolori
de dietro a un'allegria de cartapista
e passo per un celebre egoista
che se ne frega de l'umanità!

$\mathcal{T}$HE MASK

Twenty years back I went to a masquerade,
and ever since, the mask has had its place
there on the dresser, a cardboard funny face
I used to hide my own. For a long while
it stared at me with the same buffoonish smile.
One day I asked my mask point blank, "Now how
have you managed to keep your spirits high
even when I'm feeling low down,
when sit and cry is all I want to do.
You never change. You get by
without a heart. Lucky, lucky you."
But then the mask answered, "Man, what does
    complaining
do for you? Nothing. Or it gets people to saying,
'Oh, I'm so sorry! Really I am.
Poor guy! Listen, I wish there was something . . .'
But deep down, they don't give a damn.
Why don't you be like me? You can laugh.
When gladness goes and grief takes its place,
—nobody will guess—
hide your unhappiness behind my face."
So ever since that time I hide my grieving
behind a cardboard happiness
and pass for someone who couldn't care less
about the human race.

LA PUPAZZA

Quann'ero regazzino, mi' sorella,
che su per giù ciaveva l'età mia,
teneva chiusa drento a 'na scanzia
una pupazza bionna, tanto bella
Era de porcellana, e m'aricordo
che portava un bell'abbito da ballo,
scollato, co' la coda, tutto giallo,
guarnito con un bordo

Cór giraje una chiave sospirava,
moveva l'occhi, e, in certe posizzione,
pijava un'espressione
come avesse pensato a chissà che
Se chiamava Bebè

Io ce giocavo, e spesso e volentieri
la mettevo sul letto a la supina
pe' vedéje sparì l'occhioni neri
e co' la testa piena de pensieri
dicevo fra de me —Quant'è carina!
Chissà che belle cose ciavrà drento
pe' mòve l'occhi tanto ar naturale,
pe' sospirà co' tanto sentimento!—

THE DOLL

When I was just a little kid, my sister,
who was about my age,
kept a beautiful blonde doll
closed up in a glass case.
The doll was porcelain, and I remember
she wore a yellow evening gown that rustled
and swished and had a train and a low neckline
and was trimmed with ruffles.

She had a key that when you turned, she'd sigh
and move her eyes. And then she had a way
of looking at you like she was about to say
something to you, or was thinking something maybe.
Her name was Baby.

I liked to play with her, and lots of times
I'd put her down, face-up on the bed
so I could see her shut her round, black eyes,
and with a thousand thoughts swimming through my
    head,
I'd whisper to myself, "She sure is pretty!
I wonder what inner workings make her eyes
move and look at me so naturally
and put such feeling in her sighs!"

Ècchete che una sera,
nun se sa come, tutto in un momento
me sartò in testa de vedé che c'era
A mezzanotte scesi giù dal letto,
detti de guanto a un vecchio temperino
e come un assassino
je lo ficcai ner petto!
La squartai come un pollo, poverella!
ma drento nun ciaveva che una molla,
un po' de fil-de-ferro, una rotella
e un soffietto attaccato co' la colla

D'allora in poi, se vedo una regazza
che guarda e che sospira,
benanche me ce sento un tira-tira
nun me posso scordà de la pupazza

At last one night it came to me like a buzz
inside my head. I knew somehow I had
to find out what she was.
Just as midnight struck, I stole from bed, grabbed
a knife from the kitchen cutting board,
and in cold blood
stuck it against the doll's chest, and jabbed.
I opened her like a chicken, poor thing.
I searched her insides through and through, but I found
only a pulley, a rubberband, a string
to make her move, and a whistle to give her sound.

Since then, whenever I see a girl go by—
if she's pretty and has a soulful sigh,
I feel a powerful tug, but then I see
my sister's porcelain doll, looking at me.

LA MOSCA E ER RAGNO

Una Mosca diceva.—Io nun me lagno
passo la vita mia senza fa' gnente,
volo su tutto e quer che trovo magno
Se nun ce fosse er Ragno
ringrazzierei Dio Padre Onnipotente   —

Er Ragno barbottava·—Io me lamento
perché da quanno nasco insin che moro
nun me fermo un momento
e lavoro, lavoro
Dato lo stato mio
nun posso ringrazzià Dommineddio
ma bisogna, però, che riconosca
ch'ha creato la Mosca

THE SPIDER AND THE FLY

A fly was saying, "Me complain? You crazy?
Life is easy. I like being lazy.
Anywhere I light, I feast.
If spiders didn't exist,
I would be singing God's eternal praises."

A spider in turn complained: "—yes, and with cause!
All day long, from birth until I die,
I don't rest, I don't pause.
Work, work, is all I do.
So it isn't so odd
that I don't waste gratitude on God. . . .
though he did one good work I won't deny:
God did create the fly."

L'EROE A PAGAMENTO

Un vecchio Re diceva ar Generale
—Hai fatto bene a risicà la vita
pe' difenne l'onore nazzionale
Te darò la medaja
a battaja finita
—Grazzie,—fece l'eroe—ma dar contratto
devo avé cento lire per ferita
E noti bene, poi, che j'ho abbonato
un cazzotto in un occhio,
uno sgraffio ar ginocchio
e un gelone sdegnato
L'ideale?   Eh, lo so, nun c'è questione,
ma bisogna ch'io pensi a l'avvenire
nove ferite, noveccento lire,
è un prezzo d'occasione!
—Su questo qui,—rispose er Re—so' pronto
Anzi, data la somma che m'hai chiesta,
faremo mille e arrotondamo er conto
Mor'ammazzato!   —E je spaccò la testa

_A_ HERO'S PAY

A good old king was saying to his general,
"Congratulations, General, you've defended
at risk of life and limb the national honor.
I'll see you get a medal
as soon as the battle has ended."
"Thanks," said the hero, "but the contract specifies
a hundred lire per wound. You might note
that I'm not charging you for the black eyes,
the ear aches, the sore throat,
and a bad case of the shakes.
I'm all for ideals, sure, but I have to keep
my future in mind. That's what the money's for.
Nine wounds: nine hundred lire. Okay, so war
is always hell, but look, you're getting them cheap."
"No problem," said the monarch, "but instead
of the nine hundred lire you demand,
let's make it an even grand:
killed in action!" and he cut off the hero's head.

BANCHETTO

Rumori de posate,
de piatti e de bicchieri
via-vai de cammerieri,
incrocio de portate
risotto, pesce, fritto
Che pranzo! Che cuccagna!
Li tappi de sciampagna
ariveno ar soffitto,
chi parla, chi sta zitto,
chi ciancica, chi magna

Guarda laggiù la tavola
d'onore! Quanta gente!
In mezzo c'è un Ministro
che nun capisce gnente,
eppoi, de qua e de là,
tutte notorietà,
nomi più o meno cari
d'illustri fregnacciari
S'arza er Ministro e resta
in una certa posa
come pe' di' una cosa
che già s'è messa in testa
E, ner caccià le solite

Banquet

Everything smells delicious.
There's a clatter of cups and platters.
Back and forth the waiters
run with delectible dishes:
fish, pheasant, bread—
What a feast! What a spread!
Champagne keeps spilling
as corks hit the ceiling.
Someone eats while someone declares
something to someone who sits and stares.

Look up at the table of honor
where the cabinet minister sits.
He quietly eats his dinner;
he's a little dim in the wits.
If you don't mind turning to gawk
this way and that, you can see
a gaggle of prominent people
talking, talking, all talk.
The cabinet minister rises,
full of wine and bread.
His studious pose apprises
us that something's in his head.
Filling his mouth to the brim
with the resonant customary

parole rimbombanti
che j'empieno la bocca,
aggriccia l'occhi e tocca
la robba che cià avanti,
pe' dà più precisione,
a quel'idee che espone,
pe' mette più in cornice
le buggere che dice
E parla der «riscatto»
coll'indice sur piatto,
vô la «fierezza antica»
e impasta la mollica,
cercanno l'argomenti
fra tre stuzzicadenti
—La patria—dice—spera   —
E scansa la saliera
—L'Italia—dice—aspetta   —
E agguanta la forchetta
come se sventolasse una bandiera
Appena ch'ha finito
je fanno un'ovazzione
—Bravo!—Benone!—Evviva!
—Che bella affermazzione!

room-rebounding sounds,
this government dignitary
puffs his cheeks and frowns
and grips things in front of him
to steady his legs and head
and tries with a knife to spread,
thinly, a little wit
over some old horseshit.
He points toward a "National Goal"
while he fingers the finger bowl,
and "Antique Roman Virtue"
as he crumbles half a roll,
seeking a means of expressing
his thoughts in the salad dressing.
"The Fatherland, family, work!"
he intones and taps his fork.
He defends "The National Honor"
by brandishing a scallion
and waving it like an Italian
military banner.
Then everybody there
leaps wildly from his chair:
"Bravo! What an oration!
Hip, hip, hurray! Yes, yes!"

—Tutto 'sto movimento—
pensa er Ministro—prova
ch'er Popolo è contento
—Se fanno tante scene,
—barbotta er Coco—è segno
ch'hanno pranzato bene

10 marzo 1914

"This huge standing ovation
is proof," the speaker says,
"of a satisfied populace!"
"Listen to that," say the cooks—
"all that clapping!—it looks
like the pheasant scored a success!"

10 March 1914

LA FAVOLA VERA

La sera s'avvicina
e l'ombre de le cose se ne vanno
Nonna e nipote stanno
accanto a la finestra de cucina
La vecchia regge la matassa rossa
ar pupo che ingomitola la lana
er filo passa e er gnómmero s'ingrossa
—Nonna, dimme una favola   —Ciò sonno
—Quella dell'Orco che scappò sur tetto
È vero o no che l'ha ammazzato nonno?
È vero o no che venne a casa tua
una matina mentre stavi a letto?
Che te fece? la bua?
E perché se chiamava l'Orco nero?
era cattivo, è vero?
—Era giovene e bello!
—dice piano la vecchia e aggriccia l'occhi
come pe' rivedello—
Ciò ancora ne l'orecchia li tre scrocchi
che fece nonno ne l'aprì er cortello   —
La nonna pensa e regge la matassa
ar pupetto che ignómmera la lana,
se vede un'ombra è un'anima che passa
che spezza er filo rosso e s'allontana

THE TRUE FABLE

Night is about to fall,
shadows are growing, objects are getting dimmer.
Grandmother and the little boy are working
beside the kitchen window.
The old woman holds the red yarn, feeding
it out to the boy, who winds it into a ball.
The thread goes out to him. The ball gets bigger.
"Granny, tell me a story." —"I'm sleepy, child."
—"About the goblin man that Grandaddy killed.
The goblin climbed up through
the window one night. You were inside, in bed.
Were you scared? What did he do to you?
Did it hurt? What's a goblin? Was he bad?
Was he ugly? Was his face all wrong?"
"He was handsome! He was young!"
the old woman whispers, and she knits her brow
as if to see him now;
"I can still hear the three creaks the knife made
when your Grandpa pulled out the blade."
The old woman is quiet. She lets out the yarn
to the little boy, who winds it into a ball.
Across the room, a shadow seems to fall.
It cuts the thread, then flees across the lawn. . . .

A MIMÌ

Te ricordi der primo appuntamento
quanno ch'avemo inciso er nome nostro
su quela vecchia lapida der chiostro
de dietro ar cortiletto der convento?
Fui io che scrissi «Qui
Carlo baciò Mimì
Quindici maggio millenovecento »
Più de vent'anni! Pensa! Eppure, jeri,
ner rilegge quer nome e quela data,
quasi ho rimpianto l'epoca beata
che m'è costata tanti dispiaceri
e t'ho rivisto lì, come quer giorno,
coll'abbitino de setina lilla
e er cappelletto co' le rose intorno
—Tutto passa!—decevo—Le parole
che scrissi co' la punta d'una spilla
sfavilleno sur marmo, in faccia ar sole,
ma nun so' bone de rimette in vita
Una cosa finita   —
Stava pe' piagne, quanno, nun so come,
ho visto scritto su lo stesso posto
un'antra data con un antro nome
«Pasquale e Rosa li ventotto agosto
der millesettecentoventitré »
Allora ho detto —Povero Pasquale,
sta un po' peggio de me

54

To Mimi

Do you remember our first rendezvous
behind the Convent House, alone
together in the cloister? We carved
each other's name into the ancient stone.
I wrote, *Fourteen May,*
Nineteen hundred. Here Carlo kissed Mimi.
Twenty years! And yesterday
as I reread the names and the date,
I found myself regretting
the blessed, painful time that slipped away.
I saw you once more, just as you had been,
wearing a pretty lilac dress. You'd pinned
roses in your hair.
"Everything fades," I said. "Nothing can stay.
The words I chipped from marble with a knife
still glitter in the noonday sun,
but not enough: they don't bring back to life
a thing that's gone."
I stood there, feeling bad beside the wall,
when suddenly I saw another date
and other names: *Rosa and Paul,*
August twenty-eight,
seventeen hundred twenty-three.
Then I muttered to myself, "Poor Paul,
he's worse off than me."

BOLLA DE SAPONE

Lo sai ched'è la Bolla de Sapone?
L'astuccio trasparente d'un sospiro
Uscita da la canna vola in giro,
sballottolata senza direzzione,
pe' fasse cunnolà come se sia
dell'aria stessa che la porta via

Una Farfalla bianca, un certo giorno,
ner vede quela palla cristallina
che rispecchiava come una vetrina
tutta la robba che ciaveva intorno,
j'agnede incontro e la chiamò—Sorella,
fammete rimirà! Quanto sei bella!

Er cielo, er mare, l'arberi, li fiori
pare che t'accompagnino ner volo
e mentre rubbi, in un momento solo,
tutte le luci e tutti li colori,
te godi er monno e te ne vai tranquilla
ner sole che sbrilluccica e sfavilla —

La Bolla de Sapone je rispose
—So' bella, sì, ma duro troppo poco
La vita mia, che nasce per un gioco

SOAP BUBBLE

I bet you don't know what soap bubbles are.
They're nothing but the see-through skins of sighs
that issue out of little pipes and rise
and spin in aimless journeys on the air,
which cradles them as if the wind's the same
puffs of breath from which the bubbles came.

One afternoon a white butterfly
saw an airy crystal ball float past,
turning and reflecting like a glass
everything it happened to fly by.
"Dear Sister, let me look at you some more,"
she asked the bubble. "How beautiful you are!

"The sky, the sea, the flowers and the trees
seem to keep you company in flight.
How do you manage so rapidly to seize
all of the world's colors, all of its light?
You take your pleasure in the world, and on
you drift beneath the sparkle of the sun."

"I'm beautiful," the bubble said, "that's true.
But I don't last. My life, which is begun
as almost everything begins, in fun,

come la maggior parte de le cose,
sta chiusa in una goccia   Tutto quanto
finisce in una lagrima de pianto

holds up a little while, as most things do,
and finishes a drop. In fact, my dear,
it all ends in anguish and a tear."

SCIAMPAGNE

Nun bevo che Frascati Lo sciampagne
me mette in core come un'allegria
per una cosa che m'ha fatto piagne
o pe' di' mejo sento
che er piacere che provo in quer momento
è foderato de malinconia
Er botto che fa er tappo
quanno la stappo, er fiotto de la sciuma,
ch'esce, ricresce, friccica e finisce,
me rappresenta la felicità
che, appena nasce, sfuma
che, come viè sparisce

Prova ne sia che tengo sur comò
una vecchia bottija de spumante,
ma nu' la bevo e nu' la stapperò
perché me fa l'effetto che in quer vetro
ce sia riposta un po' de quela gioja
sincera e bella de tant'anni addietro
È come una riserva Forse un giorno,
combinazzione rivenisse lei,
chissà   la stapperei
pe' festeggià er ritorno,

CHAMPAGNE

All I drink now is table wine. Champagne
goes straight to my heart and makes me jolly
over whatever might have caused me pain.
I can't help thinking
the pleasure champagne gives me when I'm drinking
is only sugar-coated melancholy.
The pop the bubbles make
when I pull out the stopper, the bursting forth
of froth that flows and grows
and fizzles says how happiness at birth
begins to die,
for as it comes, it goes.

As a matter of fact, here on my window sill
I keep an old bottle of spumante.
I haven't opened it and don't think I will,
because I have a feeling this old glass
still contains some beautiful and true
joy left over from a time long passed.
I keep it in reserve. Only if at last,
against all odds, she comes back again,
I'll open it for her then
to celebrate.

ma lo spumante è un vino che svapora,
perde la forza   e allora
che figura ce faccio
se nun zompa er turaccio?

But even bottled, champagne will evaporate
and lose the force it had from holding in
And what a flop
I'll be if the cork won't pop.

LA ZAMPANA

Mentre leggevo l'urtimo volume
de la Storia d'Italia, una Zampana
sonava la trombetta intorno ar lume
Io, sur principio, nun ce feci caso
ma quanno m'è venuta sotto ar muso
pe' pizzicamme er naso,
ho preso er libbro e, paffete, l'ho chiuso

Poi l'ho riaperto subbito, e in coscenza
m'è dispiaciuto de vedella sfranta
a paggina novanta,
fra le campagne de l'Indipendenza
M'è dispiaciuto tanto che sur bordo
der fojo indove s'era apiccicata
ciò scritto 'st'epitaffio pe' ricordo

  «Qui giace una Zanzara
  che morì senza gloria,
  ma suonò la fanfara
  per restar nella Storia »

In Italia, a un dipresso,
se pô diventà celebri lo stesso

THE GNAT

As I was reading late into the night
the last volume of *The History of Italy*,
a gnat came trumpeting around my light.
At first I took no notice, but when it rose
and flitted all about my face and, damn it,
bit me on the nose,
I lifted up the history book and slammed it.

Immediately my conscience started hurting.
I opened up the book and found a smear
on page one-hundred-thirteen
right in the Campaign for Independence.
There he spread, and I wrote a rather sincere
note in the margin near where he lay flat,
an epitaph in memory of the gnat:

> Here lies a gnat. Though later ages
>   May not recall his death, he played
>   Fanfares so mighty that he made
> His mark on one of History's pages.

A person's chance for fame, however piddly,
cannot be altogether squelched in Italy.

LA VOCE DE LA COSCENZA

La sora Checca pare una balena
ogni passo che fa rìpija fiato
però sotto quer grasso esaggerato
ce sta riposta un'anima che pena
Era felice, ma la boja sorte
la fece restà vedova du' vorte

Cià avuto du' mariti, sarvognuno!
Due se n'è messi all'anima, purtroppo!
Gustavo prima e Benvenuto doppo
je so' campati dodicianni l'uno,
e adesso se li porta appennolone
attaccati a lo stesso medajone

Li tiè rinchiusi in un cerchietto d'oro
da una parte e dall'antra, sottovetro
Gustavo avanti e Benvenuto dietro,
ché così nun se vedeno fra loro
e ognuno se figura e se consola
d'esse rimpianto da una parte sola

Fa l'impressione che la vedovanza
je venga reggistrata da un controllo
perché li du' ritratti che cià ar collo

THE VOICE OF CONSCIENCE

The Widow Smith seems like a whale in a dress.
With every step she takes, her feet fall flat.
But underneath the heap of flesh and fat,
a human soul is suffering real distress.
Once she was happy. Since then she's had her slice
of bad luck: it made her a widow twice.

She had two husbands—for that, thank God in Heaven!
But both gave up the ghost and on they passed.
Alas for both. Gus first and Benny last
possessed her as a lawful wife eleven
years apiece. She carries both the men
hanging together on a single chain.

She keeps them in a gold frame, each in place
one on a side and under glass. Gus
is there in front, Benny behind him. Thus,
they never meet each other face to face.
That way she keeps her husbands satisfied:
each gets exclusive mourning on a side.

You'd think a regulation was approved
requiring equal time to mourn dead spouses,
the way the chain that holds the portraits bounces

je vanno a sbatte propio su la panza
e li mariti, cór girasse intorno,
se dànno er cambio cento vorte ar giorno

Gustavo è pensieroso e guarda storto
quasi che prevedesse l'accidente,
invece Benvenuto è soridente
come fosse contento d'esse morto,
ma ce se vede in tutt'e due la posa
de gente che sospetta quarche cosa

La sora Checca, infatti, cià er rimorso
che quann'er primo stava ancora ar monno
faceva già la scema cór seconno
in una certa cammeretta ar Corso
però je le metteva bene assai
perché Gustavo nu' lo seppe mai

Poi Benvenuto se la prese lui
—Io me te sposo subbito—je disse—
purché me giuri de nun famme er bisse
co' quarcun'antro de l'amichi tui
—Oh! fece lei—ce mancherebbe questa!
Per chi me pigli?   —E j'allisciò la testa

against her stomach every time she moves,
making the husbands toss about and sway,
changing place a hundred times a day.

Gus looks askance and seems to hold his breath,
as if he could see the next jolt coming.
Benny is all smiles. He could be humming
and really seems to be enjoying death.
Despite the differences, the portraits share
a look of suspecting something wrong somewhere.

The Widow Smith has had to bear a load
upon her mind: before death's hand beckoned
the first one, she was fooling with the second
in a small room above the Corso Road—
terribly risky, but no one raised a fuss,
and no wind of it got back to Gus.

Then it was Benny, for better or for worse.
"I'll be your husband now," he said, "and quick.
But promise me you'll never play that trick
on me with any of those friends of yours."
"Oh, you've got a lot of nerve!" she said;
"What do you take me for?" and kissed his head.

Je fu fedele? Nun garantirei,
prova ne sia ch'adesso s'è avvilita
pe' la paura che nell'antra vita
li du' mariti parlino de lei
e quanno ce s'affissa cór pensiero
je pare de sentilli pe' davero

Gustavo dice —Vojo sapé tutto!
De me che te diceva?—Ch'eri un porco
quanno partivi tu, partiva l'orco
diceva ch'eri grasso, ch'eri brutto,
che nun facevi gnente de speciale
—E invece me chiamava l'ideale!

In dodicianni, dunque, ha sempre finto!
—strilla Gustavo—Nu' l'avrei creduto!
—Abbi pazzienza —dice Benvenuto—
è stata propio lei che me cià spinto,
der resto, tu lo sai che nun so' pochi
quelli che ce facevano li giochi

Se te dovessi fa' tutta la lista!
L'avvocatino der seconno piano,
er barone, er curato, er capitano,

But was she faithful? I wouldn't take a vow
to that. In fact, she's getting gloomier,
fearing the two might be discussing her
somewhere together in the next life now.
To make things worse, whenever that thought crosses
her mind, suddenly she hears their voices:

"Tell me the truth," says Gus. "Don't spare my pride.
What did she think of me?" "That you were a pig,
that your performance wasn't worth a fig,
that you were fat and ugly, that when you died,
she felt like she'd been rescued from a beast."
"And yet she always said I was the best!"

cries Gus; "I could have sworn that she was true.
Eleven years of marriage—all a lie!"
"Take it easy," Benny says, "don't cry.
I was the one that she was lying to.
You think you were the only man she loved
to string along and make a fool of?

"I'd hate to have to count them—the physician,
the law student on the second floor,
the captain and the priest—wait, there were more—

perfino Giggi, quel'elettricista
ch'un giorno j'ha rimesso er campanello
—Pure co' quello lì?—Pure co' quello!—

'Sta voce che risente così spesso
nun è che la coscenza che lavora
su lì peccati che faceva allora
rimossi da li scrupoli d'adesso
e le scappate fatte, o belle o brutte,
una per una, le rivede tutte

Apposta soffre ché le pene sue
so' appunto li ricordi de 'sti fatti
allora se riguarda li ritratti,
pulisce er vetro, bacia tutt'e due
e, sospiranno, fiotta a denti stretti
—Ereno tanto boni, poveretti!

the judge, the baron, George, the electrician
who came to fix the doorbell for you once."
"What? Not him?" "Him, too." "Oh, I was a dunce!"

The voices in her mind that won't allow
her peace are just her conscience, which again,
again, mulls over sins committed then,
far from the scruples that she's feeling now.
Beautiful or ugly, deeds long done
parade before her mind's eye, one by one.

She suffers on purpose, because she cannot reach
those early deeds of hers except through pain.
She looks at the husbands hanging from the chain,
polishes the glass and kisses each.
She sighs and grits her teeth, holds back the tears,
and murmurs, "They were good, good men, poor
    dears."

PAROLE E FATTI

Certi Sorcetti pieni de giudizzio
s'ereno messi a rosicà er formaggio,
quanno, ner vede un Gatto de passaggio,
fecero finta de tené un comizzio
Un Sorcio, infatti, prese la parola
con un pezzo de cacio ne la gola

—Colleghi!—disse—questa è la più forte
battaja de pensiero che s'è vista
io stesso lotterò pe' la conquista
de l'ideale mio fino a la morte!
Voi pure lo farete, so' sicuro   —
Ogni Sorcetto j'arispose —Giuro!

—Fanno le cose propio ar naturale,
—disse er Miciotto—come fusse vero!
L'appetito lo chiameno Pensiero,
er formaggio lo chiameno Ideale
Ma io, però, che cio l'Istituzzione
me li lavoro tutti in un boccone

WORDS AND DEEDS

Some mice, when they suddenly saw the cat,
pretended they had not come for eating
the food on the table where they sat—
not them! They were holding a public meeting!
In fact, one mouse leapt up to speak
with cheese still sticking in his cheek:

"My fellow citizens, we are engaged
in a great war of Ideas! Never before
was such a conflict fought. And I pledge
to strive for the pure Ideal. And I declare war
on lies and such. My friends, what do you say?"
"We do, too," they cried, "hurray, hurray!"

"Convincing—all this civic zeal,"
said Puss. "But that's because *Ideas*
means *appetite* to them, and *cheese*
is what they mean by *the Ideal*.
But I'm the Law. What isn't lawful
I seize and censure by the pawful."

L'ORCO NERO
ossia
LA SINCERITÀ

C'era una vorta, quanno ancora c'era
quello ch'adesso nun se trova più,
una regazza tanto mai sincera
che trattava la gente a tu per tu
e spiattellava coraggiosamente
qualunque cosa je venisse in mente

La nonna je diceva —Lella mia,
tu sei troppo sincera e questo è bello,
ma ce vô puro un po' de furberia
in modo che te regoli er cervello,
perché nun se sa mai quer che ce tocca
quanno er pensiero sorte da la bocca

Presempio, l'Orco nero, l'antro giorno,
m'ha detto che sei bella e che je piaci,
dunque, siccome è ricco, staje intorno
e, se te bacia, lassa che te baci
faje un po' de politica e vedrai
che quarche cosa ce rimedierai —

Invece Lella, quanno annò dall'Orco,
cominciò a dije —Come sete brutto!
Me parete mezz'omo e mezzo porco!—

76

THE BOGEYMAN
or
SINCERITY

Once long ago (It must have been many years;
times have changed and what once was is not)
there lived a girl who really was sincere
with everyone, who told them what was what
and with the courage of her convictions said
anything that came into her head.

"Lily," her grandma said, "my dear granddaughter,
You're too sincere. Sincerity is fine,
but under certain circumstances, lying
is much better; it keeps the brain in order.
There isn't any telling what will happen
when you try to think with your mouth open.

"The Bogeyman, for example, the other day
told me you're beautiful—he can't resist you.
When he drops by, don't rush away;
he's very rich, go on and let him kiss you.
Be politic, and he'll be grateful; plus,
you'll bring a little profit home for us."

But when the Bogeyman came to call,
here's what she said: "My God, you're ugly! Ugh!
You're half human. The other half's a hog."

Quello ce rise e disse —Doppo tutto,
ho conosciuto un sacco de persone
che stanno ne la stessa condizzione!

—Voi, però, sete l'asso!—fece lei—
Nun ho mai visto un omo così vecchio,
grasso e peloso! Ce scommetterei
che quanno ve guardate ne lo specchio
er cristallo s'appanna pe' paura
che j'arimanga impressa la figura!

Ma che v'importa? Un omo che possiede
un portafojo gonfio com'er vostro
cià sempre quarche donna che je cede
in certi casi è bello puro un mostro!
Io stessa, se ho bisogno de bajocchi,
spalanco la manina e chiudo l'occhi

—Perché nun me fai fa' l'esperimento?
—je chiese l'Orco che capiva a volo
e cacciò fòra tre pappiè da cento—
Nun te darò che un bacio, un bacio solo
—Accetto!—fece lei che stava all'erta
coll'occhi chiusi e la manina aperta

78

The Bogeyman just laughed: "Well, after all,
I'm not the only one, you must admit,
that your description could be said to fit."

"Yeah, but you! You really take the cake.
I've never seen a man who had a face
so brutish, hairy, wrinkled, fat—you'd break
the mirror if the surface didn't glaze
every time it felt you coming past,
for fear your face might print itself in glass.

"What's that to you, though? Any man who's got
as much money as you have surely might
find a woman willing to be bought.
Even a troll looks good in the right light—
even to me; when I need toys, I put
my hand out and I keep my eyes shut."

"Try me, then. Why not? See how it feels,"
the monster said, who didn't want to miss
his chance, and flashed three hundred-dollar bills.
"One kiss is all I ask. One little kiss!"
"Sure! You've got a deal!" the girl replied
with her eyes shut and both hands opened wide.

Senza da' tempo ar tempo, l'Orco nero
j'annò vicino e sospirò tre vorte
—Doppo 'sto bacio tornerò com'ero,
doppo 'sto bacio cambierò la sorte
ecco   mó te lo do   tesoro mio!
—È fatto?—Ho fatto!—Ringrazziamo Iddio!—

Appena ch'ebbe dette 'ste parole
Lella aprì l'occhi e se trovò davanti
un giovenotto bello come er sole
cór manto e la corona de brillanti
e, da un bastone che ciaveva in mano,
capì che se trattava d'un Sovrano

Dice —Dormo o sto sveja? È un sogno, forse?—
E quasi nun credesse all'occhi sui
attastò er Re, ma quanno che s'accorse
ch'annava per attasti puro lui,
incominciò a strillà —Le mano a casa!   —
pe' fa' capì che s'era persuasa

—Scusa,—je disse er Re—ma so' cent'anni
ch'aspetto 'sto momento, e fino a che
una donna sincera e senza inganni

Not wasting any time, the Bogeyman
stepped nearer to the girl and breathed three sighs:
"With this one kiss, my life begins again.
With this one kiss, I'll be the man I was!
Here! This kiss is yours. My precious one!"
"You finished?" "Yes, I have." "I'm glad that's done!"

When she had said these words, which were the truth,
Lily looked, and inches from her nose
there stood a tall, resplendent, handsome youth
with a diamond crown and diamond studded clothes,
and from the scepter she could clearly see
the man she was dealing with was royalty.

"Am I awake? I can't believe my eyes!"
she said, and, just to see if he was real,
she touched the King, but when she realized
the king was meaning to return the feel,
she screamed, "Okay! No more handsies, Prince!"
That way she let him know she was convinced.

"Sorry," he said. "It's been a hundred years
I've waited for this moment. Without one
good lady, with a voice sincere and clear

nun me parlava chiaro come te,
sarei rimasto brutto come un diavolo
e invece d'esse Re nun ero un cavolo

Fu doppo una congiura de Palazzo
che venni sequestrato da l'Orchesse
ar posto mio ce méssero un pupazzo
perché la gente nun se n'accorgesse,
e me fecero fa' l'omo servatico
per via d'un certo imbrojo dipromatico

Adesso che m'hai rotto l'incantesimo
levo er pupazzo e me ripijo er trono
Sarò chiamato Mardoccheo ventesimo
fijo de Mardoccheo decimonono
e, se tu pure approverai l'idea,
diventerai Reggina Mardocchea

Ma prima, dimme hai fatto mai l'amore?
t'hanno baciato quela bocca santa?—
Lella s'aricordò d'un senatore
che l'aveva baciata tutta quanta
stava quasi pe' dijelo, però
ripensò ar trono e j'arispose —No!

as yours, speaking the truth as you have done
today, I'd still be uglier than garbage.
I wouldn't be a king. I'd be a cabbage.

"An evil palace plot was my undoing.
I got closed up behind a monster's face.
The plotters propped a puppet up in place
of me to keep the populace from knowing,
then struck a diplomatic deal and managed
to pass me off as some ignoble savage.

"But now that, thanks to you, the spell is burst,
I'm going to prise that puppet from the throne.
I'll be King Macheroan the Twenty-first,
son of the twentieth King Macheroan,
and you shall be my Queen Macheroanea,
that is, if you like the idea.

"But first, have you had any other lovers?
Those sacred lips of yours—have they been touched?"
It did occur to Lily that there was
one senator who'd kissed her rather much,
and was about to tell him so. However,
she thought about the throne and answered, "Never!"

LA SCENATA DER SIGNORINO

Se so' lasciati jeri La Contessa
l'è venuto a trovà verso le sei
—Mario, nun t'amo più!—j'ha detto lei —
S'avemo da lascià stasera stessa   —

Lui j'ha risposto —Ah, cinica che sei!
Forse c'è un antro   Dimmelo! Confessa!
—Oh—dice—questo   poco t'interessa
e, benché fosse, non te lo direi   —

A 'ste parole er signorino ha pianto
—Ecco—j'ha detto—er sogno che svanisce!
Povero core mio che soffre tanto!—
Faceva pena! Invece quela strega
lo sai che j'ha risposto?—*Ge m'anfisce*   —
che in francese vô di' chi se ne frega!

MY YOUNG LORD'S SCENE

They broke up yesterday. She did it right;
she came by here to tell him: "Mario,
I don't love you anymore. You know
it was over between us last night."

"How could you be so false?" he said to her.
"There must be someone else. Tell me his name!"
"Him? Not your concern. And all the same,
I wouldn't tell you even if it were."

That's when my young lord broke down and cried:
"The dearest dream I ever had has died!
My poor heart! What am I going to do?"
A stone would've wept. I did. But her? That witch—
know what her answer was? "*Jemon fitch*"!
That's French. It means, "Who gives a screw?"

ER CONSUMO DE LA FEDE

Quer San Pietro de bronzo che se vede
drento San Pietro, co' la chiave in mano,
a furia de baciallo, piano piano
j'hanno magnato più de mezzo piede

E quella è tutta gente che ce crede
perché devi pensà ch'ogni cristiano,
ch'ariva da vicino o da lontano
lo logra co' li baci de la fede

Però c'è un sampietrino che m'ha detto
come er consumo pô dipenne pure
che lo vanno a pulì cór fazzoletto
Ma questo qua nun sposta la questione
e, a parte quele poche fregature,
è un gran trionfo pe' la religgione

THE CONSUMMATION OF FAITH

You know that big bronze statue of Saint Pete
inside Saint Peter's, holding up the keys?
Crowds of Christians falling on their knees
and kissing him have nibbled bit by bit

half his foot off. Who'd have thought so many
believers from far and near with lips of faith
could come and kiss a foot of bronze in half?
But look at the stump. It stands as testimony.

Well . . . there's another cause for Saint Pete's club:
all that wiping with a handkerchief
every time devout lips kiss him,
or so Saint Peter's sexton claims. But if
we don't quibble at every little rub,
it's a triumph for Catholicism!

LISA E MOLLICA

I

Se voleveno bene Dio sa quanto,
eppure nun annaveno d'accordo
perché Mollica, ch'era mezzo sordo,
l'accompagnava e nun sentiva er canto

In quela voce piena de rimpianto
c'era la cantilena d'un ricordo
ma chi capiva? Er pubbrico balordo
li minchionava e ce rideva tanto

—Manna, Mollica! Facce un pezzo bello!—
E'r vecchio pizzicava la chitara
mentre Lisa attaccava un ritornello
—Inverno o estate, autunno o primavera,
quann'una canta co' la bocca amara
nun c'è più gnente che je dice spera!—

LISA AND COOKY

I

Heaven only knows how old and strong
their love is. Still they never harmonize;
Cooky is half-deaf. But he tries;
whenever Lisa sings, he plays along.

Beneath the tremor in her voice there lies
an anquish buried in an old-time ditty,
which the public—what do they know of pity?—
jeers and hoots and doesn't recognize.

"Hit it, Cooky! Go to it!" they bellow.
The old guitarist picks out his chords,
and Lisa sings a little ritornella:
"Winter, spring and summer, fall and winter,
you try to sing, but when you have a bitter
taste in your mouth, you don't hear the words."

II

Un giorno che giraveno cór piatto
Lisa me disse —Se m'avesse vista
quanno facevo la canzonettista
caro signore, diventava matto¹

Dijelo, Mollica   —Er chitarista
approvò co' la testa, soddisfatto,
eppoi me disse —Guardi 'sto ritratto
ch'uscì in quer tempo sopra una rivista   —

E cacciò fòra un pezzo de giornale
indove c'era la fotografia
d'Isa Pupè, «l'eccentrica mondiale»
—Allora nun avevo che vent'anni¹
—sospirò Lisa co' malinconia—
Ma se m'avesse vista sottopanni¹

II

Once, as they passed the plate around, she said,
"If you had seen me when I was the rage,
singing on every dance hall stage,
Sir, you would have gone off your head.

"Wouldn't he have, Cooky?" The old picker
nodded—you could see his face light up.
"That's right," he said. "Look, they had a write-up
about her in a magazine, with a picture!"

Then he pulled out an old newspaper page
And pointed to the photo. The caption read,
"Isa Pupe, Free Spirit of the West."
"There I am, just twenty years of age!"
She looked at the picture, sighed, and shook her head:
"But you should have seen me underneath the dress!"

III

Mollìca, dillo tu com'ero grassa   —
Subbito er vecchio, che beveva er vino,
scrocchiò la lìngua come un vetturino
mentre se pizzicava la ganassa

—Perché saranno ormai vent'anni e passa
che conosco Mollica! Era destino
Cantavo ne lo stesso teatrino
dove che lui sonava la grancassa

M'insegnava la musica, e a le prove
portava la chitara espressamente
pe' ripassamme le canzone nove
Daje e ridaje, me se mise intorno
però in quer tempo nun successe gnente
ché, purtroppo, ero vergine Ma un giorno

III

"Tell him, Cooky, wasn't I a dish?"
Cooky, who was drinking, put his wine back,
clicked the way the driver of a hack
speaks to his horse, and then he went, "Whoosh!"

"You see," she said. "It's twenty years and some
since Cooky and I met. It was fate;
there was this place where I worked late
singing and Cooky played the bass drum.

"He came to all the rehearsals and brought along
his old guitar. Know why he did? He'd play
for me and teach me the latest songs.
He was always at my beck and call.
Lot of good it did him—after all,
I was still a virgin. But one day . . .

IV

Doppo tre mesi, come vorse Iddio
fui scritturata a Genova Ciannai
Ma a lassà Roma me dispiacque assai
massimamente pe' Mollica mio

Partii de notte Venne a dimme addio
—Sta' attenta a te,—me fece—e caso mai   —
Cominciò a piagne Dico —Ma che fai!
Quanto sei scemo!—E un po' piansi pur'io

In tutt'er viaggio me pareva che
quele parole fussero restate
ner rumore der treno Attenta a te .
Attenta a te! Ma dice bene quello
quanno se nasce pecore segnate
o prima o poi s'ha da finì ar macello —

IV

"With God's help, I finally got a booking,
a nightclub up in Genoa. I signed
and left. I hated leaving my friends behind
in Rome, but most, it hurt me leaving Cooky.

"I left at night. He came to say goodbye:
'Take care of yourself. Some day—' and he starts crying!
'Cooky!' I say, 'what's this? What are you trying
to do? Silly! Now you're making me cry.'

"All that long trip north I couldn't help
hearing those words playing and replaying
in the sound of the tracks: 'Take care of yourself . . .
Take care of yourself.' Yeah, but the old saying
I used to hear is true: *Sooner or later*
the lamb that's marked is sure to go to slaughter."

V

E Lisa riallacciò con un sospiro
er ricordo d'un fatto ormai lontano,
quanno s'unì con un fachiro indiano
che cercò de giocaje un brutto tiro

Dice —Deve sapé che 'sto fachiro,
che invece era un barbiere de Milano,
aveva combinato tutto un piano
cór solo scopo de portamme in giro

Per mesi e mesi, stupida che fui
ho lavorato ne l'esperimenti
vestita da odalisca, assieme a lui
In uno me legava li capelli
e, mentre me teneva co' li denti,
faceva er gioco de li tre cortelli —

V

Lisa sighed a little, then unearthed
another memory: an Indian fakir
teamed up with her. He had in mind to take her
up and down Italy for all she was worth.

"But," she said, "I wouldn't want you thinking
this fakir was real. A barber from Milan
is all he was. He cooked up our two-man
routine for one reason, and that was stringing

"me along. For months—I was such a jerk—
I danced to his tune and worked in his act
got up like him in a turban like a Turk.
In one routine he tied my hair back,
gripped me by the teeth and with three quick
flicks of his wrist, performed the three-knife trick."

VI

Allora Lisa me spiegò com'era
che ciaveva la voce rovinata
—Fu lo spavento d'una cortellata
che me dette er fachiro quela sera

Pe' potello sarvà da la galera
detti a d'intenne ch'ero scivolata
Ma guardi qua, che sfrizzola m'ha data!—
E se slacciò la camicietta nera

—So' sedici anni e ancora se conosce   —
E mise er deto ne la cicatrice
che se sperdeva tra le pelle flosce
Mollica disse —Se me dava retta
nun succedeva, povera infelice!—
E je riabbottonò la camicetta

VI

Lisa laughed and went on to instruct me
on why it was her vocal chords were shot:
"I haven't sung right since the shock I got
on the night the fakir's knife struck me.

"I didn't want him locked in some jailhouse,
so I let on he only scratched the skin,
but the skin's still scarred where the knife went in.
Look here!" And she opened up her blouse.

"Sixteen years it's been, and it still shows."
She put her finger on her chest and rubbed
the scar to where it vanished in the folds
of pale flesh. "If she'd done me right, poor kid,
things wouldn't have gone the way they did,"
said Cooky, and buttoned Lisa's blouse back up.

VII

In quer momento, da la commitiva
d'un gruppo de signori e de signore
uno strillò —Volemo er professore!
Musica, sor peloso! Evviva, evviva!   —

Una biondina disse —Per favore,
ce vorebbe cantà la «Casta diva»?
—La «Norma»?—chiese Lisa—e chi ciariva?
Quarche stornello sì, co' tutto er core   —

E incominciò a cantà —Fiore de menta,
in mezzo ar petto ancora ciò l'impronta
de la passione mia che me tormenta
—Brava!—je disse l'oste—nun te resta
che de faje la mossa!—E Lisa, pronta,
arzò la cianca e se sgrullò la vesta

VII

Just as he finished speaking, from the last row
of little tables in the dive, some jester
shouted, "Hey! Let's hear it from the professor!
Eviva, eviva! Music, music, Maestro!"

A young blonde woman said, "I have a request:
Would you sing the 'Casta Diva,' please?"
"From *Norma*?" Lisa asked, "Who could hit those
notes? How about a stornello? I'll give it my best."

She started singing: "Flower of the mint . . .
The place above my heart still holds the print
of the old passion, where it still hurts."
"Bravo," said the tavern keeper, "now quick,
do your stuff for them." Then Lisa kicked
her knee up high and shook her lifted skirts.

ER SONATORE AMBULANTE

Ogni tanto veniva in trattoria
pe' sonà quer violino strappacore
che quanno nun raschiava er «Trovatore»
martirizzava la «Cavalleria»

Successe che una sera, un avventore,
je disse —Basta, co' 'sta zinfonia!
perché ciai rotto l'anima! Va' via!
Sempre una lagna! Brutto scocciatore!—

Ner sentì 'ste parole, er violinista,
radica vera de baron futtuto,
j'incominciò a sonà l'inno fascista
Allora l'avventore, rassegnato,
arzò la mano in segno de saluto
ma sottovoce disse —M'hai fregato!

STREET MUSICIAN

Every night, there at the tavern door he
appears with bow and fiddle. Without a pause he
chins the fiddle, crooks his elbow, saws the
Cavalleria, martyrs the *Trovatore*.

At last one day a customer ups and shouts,
"You trying to break our hearts or break our ears?
I'm telling you I've had it up to here
with all your screeping and scraping. Get out!

"No more of your wheezing sob songs, damn them."
That old flimflam man, the Boss Futoots,
must have been the violist's dad,
because he quick strikes up the Fascist Anthem
to which the customer leaps up, salutes,
and underneath his breath swears, "I've been had."

SOGNO BELLO

I

—Macché!—je disse subbito er dottore—
Qui nun se tratta mica d'anemia!
È gravidanza, signorina mia
soliti incertarelli de l'amore!—

Pe' Mariettina fu una stretta ar core
—So' rovinata! Vergine Maria!
Madonna santa, fate che nun sia!
Nun potrei sopportà 'sto disonore!—

Ma appena vidde ch'era propio vero
corse da Nino —Nun è gnente!—dice—
Se leveremo subbito er pensiero
Ce vò la puncicata Domatina
te porto da 'na certa levatrice
che già l'ha fatto a un'antra signorina —

$\mathcal{J}$HE GOOD DREAM

I

"What'd you expect? What you've got has nothing
to do with virus or anemia. This
is pregnancy," the doctor told her, "Miss,
the usual unforeseen effect of loving."

These words struck Marietta like a stake
straight through her heart: "Mary, Virgin, no!
Sweet Mother, make it so it isn't so.
Please. The shame is more than I can take."

When she was certain what he said was true,
she ran in a panic to tell Nino, too.
"Easy," he said. "A little puncture'll do it.
If we move fast, there's really nothing to it.
We'll go tomorrow to a midwife who
I know once did it to a girl I knew."

II

La sera Mariettina agnede a letto
coll'occhi gonfi e con un gnocco in gola,
e s'anniscose sott'a le lenzola
pe' piagne zitta, senza da' sospetto

Poi pijò sonno e s'insognò un pupetto
che je diceva —Se te lascio sola,
povera mamma mia, chi te consola
quanno t'invecchierai senza un affetto?—

E, sempre in sogno, je pareva come
se er fijo suo crescesse a l'improviso
e la baciava e la chiamava a nome
Allora aperse l'occhi adacio adacio
e s'intese una bocca accanto ar viso,
che la baciava co' lo stesso bacio

II

That night when Marietta went to bed
with her eyes puffed up and her throat tied
into a knot, she hid in the sheets and tried
to cry so her sobs couldn't be heard.

At last she slept. A little kid was there,
Saying, "Momma, if I leave you, who
is going to be around to care for you
after you get old and no one cares?"

Then somehow Marietta had the feeling
her son was growing. And she felt him bent
over the bed. Then she could hear him calling
her by name. Her eyelids started flicking
open slowly. Slowly she was waking
to more kisses. And they were the same she dreamt.

III

Era la madre —Mamma, mamma bella!—
E se la strinse ar petto —Amore santo!
Che t'insognavi che parlavi tanto
e facevi la bocca risarella?

Però ciai l'occhi come avessi pianto
Dimme? che t'è successo?—E pe' vedella
più mejo in faccia, aprì la finestrella
e fece l'atto de tornaje accanto

S'intese un fischio —Mamma! questo è lui
che sta aspettanno sotto l'arberata
Dije che vada pe' li fatti sui
Anzi faje capì che se l'onore
se pô sarvà con una puncicata
preferisco de dajela ner core

III

It was her mother. "Mamma!" "Yes, child,"
her mother answered as the daughter clung
close to her; "you must have had a long,
sweet dream the way you talked in your sleep and
   smiled.

"What's this? What's this? Your face and cheeks are wet.
Marietta, tell me what's the matter."
She stood up from the bed, pulled back the shutter
and turned her face to the light to see her better.

There was a whistle outside. "Mamma, that's him!
Standing underneath an oak tree limb.
Tell him to mind his business, go away!
Or better—tell him if the only way
he can save honor's with an art-
ful little puncture, I'll put it in his heart!"

ALL'OMBRA

Mentre me leggo er solito giornale
spaparacchiato all'ombra d'un pajaro,
vedo un porco e je dico —Addio, majale¹—
vedo un ciuccio e je dico —Addio, somaro¹—

Forse 'ste bestie nun me caperanno,
ma provo armeno la soddisfazzione
de potè di' le cose come stanno
senza paura de finì in priggione

In The Shade Of A Hay Rick

I read my paper, back propped against the hay.
Here comes a hog, so I look up and say,
"Goodbye, pig!" And then across the grass
here comes a donkey; I say, "Goodbye, ass!"

No way of telling if they've understood.
Whether they have or not, it does me good
to call things what they are without the dread
of having to go to jail for what I've said.

LA FINE DELL'ORCO

Le Favole oramai stanno in ribbasso
a principià dar Mago e la Strega,
che chiusero bottega,
puro le Fate so' rimaste a spasso
e vanno in compagnia de la Befana
che je fa da mezzana
Perfino l'Orco, quello
che prima se magnava in un boccone
li regazzini vivi
quann'ereno cattivi,
adesso è diventato un bonaccione
nun mette più paura
a nessuna cratura
Anzi, la notte, spesso je succede
che vede in sogno tutto quer ch'ha fatto
e allora fiotta, soffia come un gatto,
e piagne in bona fede
Ma l'orchessa, che dorme cór marito,
quanno sente 'ste buggere je strilla
—Finiscela de piagne, arimbambito¹
sennò   chiamo un balilla¹

THE LAST OF THE BOGEYMAN

Fairytales have suffered a huge drop
in popularity. First the Wolf, then the Wizard
closed up shop.
Then the three cruel Sisters were out of a job,
along with the mean
old Witch and then the Wicked Queen.
Even the Bogeyman,
the guy who chewed
children up or gulped them live and whole
if they were rude,
is now considered just a good old soul.
Even babies in the pen
aren't afraid of bogeymen.
Now it's the Bogeyman who hears
and sees in dreams things he once did,
then hisses like a cat, and screams in bed,
and sobs real tears.
But then his wife, the Bogeywoman, dashes in
to her bogeyhusband in the sheets and yells,
"What's this fuss? Shut up that noise, or else,
you damn crybaby, I'll call a Boy Fascist in!"

Matina Abbonora

Doppo una notte movimentatella
ritorno a casa che s'è fatto giorno
Già s'apreno le chiese. l'aria odora
de matina abbonora e scampanella
Sbadijo e fumo ciò l'idee confuse
e la bocca più amara de l'assenzio
Casco dar sonno Le persiane chiuse
coll'occhi bassi guardeno in silenzio
Solo m'ariva da lontano assai,
er ritornello d'una cantilena
de quela voce che nun scordo mai
—Ritorna presto, sai?
Sennò me pijo pena   —

E vedo una vecchietta
che sospira e m'aspetta

EARLY MORNING

After a wild little night out on the town
I go on home. After all, it's day.
Already the churches are opening. The smells
of early morning fill the air. Bells
are ringing everywhere. I yawn and smoke. My mind's
grown fuzzy, and the taste of absinthe parches
my tongue and throat. With lowered lids the blinds
watch me stumble past. I'm not home yet.
Suddenly I hear, from far off, snatches
of an old refrain from a song
in a voice I don't forget:
"Hurry home soon. Please, don't stay out long.
If you do, you know I'll worry."

And I see
an old woman still waiting up for me.

ABBITUDINE

Er giorno stesso che la Capinera
fu fatta priggioniera,
ingabbiata che fu,
non volle cantà più
E disse —Come posso
restà lontana dar boschetto mio
dove ciò er nido su l'abete rosso?
—Ringrazzia Iddio che nun t'è annata peggio,
—trillò un Canario che je stava accanto—
pur'io, sur primo ciò sofferto tanto
ma poi ripresi subbito er gorgheggio
E mó, piuttosto che schiattà de rabbia
m'adatto a fa' li voli su misura
Me bevo er Celo e canto a la Natura
che vedo tra li ferri de la gabbia

*F*ORCE OF HABIT

From the very moment when the linnet
was snared, then caged and kept, her wings hemmed in,
she lost her spirit,
and she couldn't sing.
She said, "How can I ever
get used to being here, far from my forest,
where I have my nest, high in a red fir?"
"Cheer up. Cheer up. Thank God it isn't worse,"
trilled the canary in the cage next door.
"I was like you, dying from grief at first,
but then I picked up where I'd sung before.
At last instead of choking on my rage,
I learned to adapt. Now I take measured flights,
drink in the sky and sing to what's in sight
out there between the wires of my cage."

ER DESTINO

Una notte er Destino,
mentre se scatenava un temporale,
pensò de ariparasse sotto a un pino
Ma, appena vidde che da piedi all'arbero
c'era ingrufata un'Aquila Reale,
se sgrullò l'acqua e seguitò er cammino
—No,—disse—vado via
perché, se per disdetta
Giove scaraventasse una saetta,
potrebbero pensà ch'è córpa mia

DESTINY

One night, as it was raining
on the road where Destiny happened to be,
Destiny paused, as she considered running
for shelter beneath a tall pine tree.
But when she saw the Roman Eagle bristle
underneath the tree, she paused again,
shook off the drops, and walked on through the drizzle.
"Oh no, no," said the immortal dame,
"Because if by dùmb luck,
Jove's thunderbolt struck,
I'd be the one for sure to get the blame."

PRESUNZIONI

La luna piena che inargenta l'orto
è più granne der solito direi
che quasi se la gode a rompe l'anima
a le cose più piccole de lei

E la Lucciola, forse, nun ha torto
se chiede ar Grillo —Che maniera è questa?
Un po' va bè' però stanotte esaggera!—
E smorza el lume in segno de protesta

PRESUMPTION

The full moon, spreading silver on the lawn,
is huger than she usually is. She's either
inconsiderate, or she likes to break
the hearts of little creatures underneath her.

The lightning bug, complaining to the cricket,
has a point. He asks, "What's going on?
Enough's enough. She doesn't have to show off!"
Then as an act of protest, he shuts his glow off.

DISINTERESSE

Disse un Porco a la Quercia·—Tu sei grande,
forte e potente! È tanto che t'ammiro¹
—Lo so   —rispose lei con un sospiro—
è un pezzo che t'ingrassi co' le ghiande

DISINTEREST

The pig said to the oak, "You're big and strong
and mighty. I'm impressed with you for that."
"I know," sighed the oak. "I've watched you for a long
while down there, eating acorns, getting fat."

Lo SCIALLETTO

Cor venticello che scartoccia l'arberi
entra una foja in cammera da letto
È l'inverno che ariva e, come ar solito,
quanno passa de qua, lascia un bijetto
Jole, infatti, me dice —Stammatina
me vojo mette quarche cosa addosso
nun hai sentito ch'aria frizzantina?—
E cava fôri lo scialetto rosso,
che sta riposto fra la naftalina

—M'hai conosciuto proprio co' 'sto scialle
te ricordi?—me chiede e, mentre parla,
se l'intorcina stretto su le spalle—
S'è conservato sempre d'un colore
nun c'è nemmeno l'ombra d'una tarla¹
Bisognerebbe ritrovà un sistema,
pe' conservà così pure l'amore   —

E Jole ride, fa l'indiferente
ma se sente la voce che je trema

THE SHAWL

A gust of wind comes rushing from the yard.
It rakes the trees, swings back the bedroom door,
and here's a leaf. That's Winter back in town.
Whenever he comes back, he leaves his card.
Now Julie says, "This morning I should draw
something over my shoulders for the chill.
Don't you feel the weather's gotten raw?"
At that she rummages in the room until
she pulls from a chest her charming red shawl.

"This is the shawl I wore the day you met me.
Do you remember?" She twists the red cloth
around her neck and shoulders as she's speaking.
"Look, the color's just as bright as ever
and not even the shadow of a moth.
We need someone to figure out a clever
technique for keeping love intact, too."

Then Julie laughs, as if she's only joking,
but all the same, I hear her voice quaver.

CORTILE

Li panni stessi giocano cór vento
tutti felici d'asciugasse ar sole
zinali, sottoveste, bavarole,
fasce, tovaje   Che sbandieramento!
Su, da la loggia, una camicia bianca
s'abbotta d'aria e ne l'abbottamento
arza le braccia ar celo e le spalanca
Pare che dica —Tutt'er monno è mio!—
Ma, appena er vento cambia direzzione,
gira, se sgonfia, resta appennolone
E un fazzoletto sventola l'addio

COURTYARD

A wild wind's in the courtyard. The clothes and rags
are playing, drying in the sun and air.
Tablecloths and towels and underwear,
napkins, diapers, bibs—what a flapping of flags!
A white shirt, high on a gallery clothesline
swells with a sweep of air and in its swell
reaches for the sky with outstretched wrists,
seems to be shouting, "All the world is mine!"
for just one moment, then, with the wind's shift, twists,
deflates, settles down, and sags . . .
and a handkerchief waves farewell.

EPIGRAMMA

Roma de travertino,
refatta de cartone,
saluta l'imbianchino,
suo prossimo padrone

EPIGRAM

Rome, made from marble,
rebuilt with cardboard,
salutes the house painter,
her next landlord.

CAFFÈ DEL PROGRESSO

Er Caffè del Progresso
è un bottega bassa, così scura
ch'ogni avventore è l'ombra de se stesso
Nessuno fiata Tutti hanno paura
de di' un pensiero che nun è permesso

Perfino la specchiera,
tutt'ammuffita da l'ummidità,
è diventata nera
e nun respecchia più la verità

Io stesso, quanno provo
de guardamme ner vetro
me cerco e nun me trovo

Com'è amaro l'espresso
ar Caffè der Progresso!

1938

THE CAFE DEL PROGRESSO

The Cafe del Progresso,
is a hole in a cellar wall
so dark the customer stands in his own shade.
No one breathes. Everyone's afraid
of saying something that's against the law.

Even the mirror that hangs behind the bar
is smeared from all the damp
with mold and doesn't mirror
things the way they are.

I've got to admit even I,
when I look and try
to see myself, I can't . . .

You get to hate the espresso
in the Cafe der Progresso!

1938

LA GUIDA

Quela Vecchietta ceca, che incontrai
la notte che me spersi in mezzo ar bosco,
me disse —Se la strada nu' la sai,
te ciaccompagno io, ché la conosco

Se ciai la forza de venimme appresso,
de tanto in tanto te darò una voce
fino là in fonno, dove c'è un cipresso,
fino là in cima, dove c'è la Croce   —

Io risposi —Sarà   ma trovo strano
che me possa guidà chi nun ce vede   —
La Ceca, allora, me pijò la mano
e sospirò —Cammina!—
            Era la Fede

1942

132

THE GUIDE

The old blind woman I met as I wandered through
the night when I was lost in the dark wood,
said to me, "If you don't know the road,
I'll go along with you, because I do.

"If you have the strength, stay close. I'll be at hand.
Listen for me on the road as it takes you
down to the depths: there a cypress stands;
up to the heights: there a cross awaits you."

"All right," I said, "but I don't see what good
you can do guiding if you can't see the woods."
The old blind woman, who didn't waste time talking,
was Faith. She took my hand and sighed, "Start
    walking."

1942

CHIAROSCURA

Giustizzia, Fratellanza, Libbertà
Quanta gente ridice 'ste parole!
Ma chi le vede chiare? Iddio lo sa!
Er Gallo canta quanno spunta er sole,
Er Gufo canta ne l'oscurità

1944

LIGHT AND DARK

Freedom, Brotherhood, Justice, Right—
people often say the words!
But who can clearly see the things?
When morning breaks, it's the cock that sings.
The owl sings at night.

1944

FELICITÀ

C'è un Ape che se posa
su'un bottone de rosa
lo succhia e se ne va
Tutto sommato, la felicità
è una piccola cosa

HAPPINESS

A bee settled
on a rose petal.
It sipped, and off it flew.
All in all, happiness, too
is something little.

Notes

4/5. "Er ventriloco" ("Ventriloquist") is the first poem in Trilussa's collected works (*Tutte le poesie*, Milan: Mondadori, 1951).

24/25. "Core de tigre" ("Tiger's Heart"). See York's famous rebuke of Queen Margaret in Part III of Shakespeare's *King Henry the Sixth* (I, iv, 137): "O tiger's heart, wrapt in woman's hide!"

38/39. "La pupazza" ("The Doll"). Unlike the narrator of this poem, Trilussa did not have a sister.

102/103. "Er sonatore ambulante" ("Street Musician"). Baron Futtuto (Boss Futoots) is the vulgar name for the proverbial unscrupulous political con man. Belli mentions him in his sonnets, and his reputation evidently reached beyond Rome, for my friend Johnny Danti remembers the name from his childhood in Florence.

112/113. "La fine dell'Orco" ("The Last of the Bogeyman"). "The most renowned [of the boy Fascist] formations were the Balilla for boys ages eight to fourteen, named after the legendary Genoese streetboy whose rock-throwing exploits against the city's Austrian occupiers in 1746 were cited as an exemplary display of heroic protonationalism." (Victoria De Grazia, in *Historical Dictionary of Fascist Italy*, ed. Philip V. Cannistraro, Westport, Conn. Greenwood Press, 1982, 569)

114/115. "Matina abbonora" ("Early Morning"). Trilussa's mother had died many years earlier, in 1912. (Trilussa's father had been dead since 1874.)

118/119. "Er Destino" ("Destiny"). The Fascists often bragged about being on "The path of destiny." The royal eagle was emblematic of the Italian nation.

128/129 "Epigramma" ("Epigram") From Luigi Barzini's *The Italians*, (New York Atheneum, 1964, 81) Barzini writes, "Rome was made to appear more modern, wealthy, and powerful with the addition of whole cardboard buildings, built like film sets, on the occasion of Hitler's visit, in 1938, in the fashion of the Potemkin's villages (Trilussa, the dialect poet, wrote a famous epigram on the occasion) Hitler was notoriously impressed" The lines proved sadly prophetic on September 23, 1943, when, two weeks after the promise that Rome would be left an open city under Italian command and a few days after the reinstatement of Mussolini's failed dictatorship, German troops marched into Rome and arrested and deported the Italian military commanders there

130/131 "Caffe del Progresso" ("The Cafe del Progresso") The shift from the Italian *del* (of the) in the title and the first line to the harsher Romanesco *der* at the end is intentional

132/133 "La Guida" ("The Guide") In *Illustrissimi* (tr by William Weaver [Boston Little, Brown, 1978]), Albino Luciani (Pope John Paul I) reproves Trilussa for being less impassioned than Saint Augustine "in describing his journey toward faith" (p 30), which, he informs Trilussa, is "not the pathetic walk along the path in the woods, but a journey at times difficult, at times dramatic, and always mysterious" (p 29) Luciani ignores the allusions in the poem, both literary and historical The opening lines, echoing in Romanesco the opening lines of *The Inferno*, point to Rome in 1942 as a hell where faith is as difficult as at any time in its history Trilussa adds the date to the bottom of the poem to keep later readers from missing the point (Trilussa is the only contemporary writer whom the future Pope addresses in his letters The only other Italian poets he mentions are Petrarch and Belli)

136/137 "Felicita" ("Happiness") Perhaps the most popular of all Trilussa's poems, this is the last in the Mondadori edition

Selected Bibliography

Barzini, Luigi. *The Italians*. New York: Atheneum, 1964.

Belli, G. G. *I sonetti*, ed. Maria Teresa Lanza, introduced by Carlo Muscetta. Milan: Feltrinelli, 1965.

———. *Sonnets of Giuseppi Belli* (bilingual), tr. and introduced by Miller Williams. Baton Rouge: LSU Press, 1981

Maria Teresa Russo "Trilussa senatore," in *Studi trilussiani*, Rome: Istituto di Studi Romani, 1973, pp. 225–37

Trilussa. *Poesie Scelte*, ed. Pietro Gibellini. Milan: Mondadori, 1969.

———. *Tutte le poesie*, ed. Pietro Pancrazi. Milan: Mondadori, 1951.

Vaccaro, Gennaro. *Vocabolario romanesco trilussiano*. Rome: Romana Libri Alfabeto, 1971.

For a comprehensive bibliography before 1978, see Anne-Christine Faitrop, *Trilussa: doppio volto di un uomo e di un'opera*, Rome: Istituto di Studi Romani, 1979.